C000124902

A BOOT UP

THE NORTHUMBERLAND COAST

Anthony Toole

First published in Great Britain in 2010

British Library Cataloguing-in-Publication Data
A CIP record for this title is available from the British Library

ISBN 978 0 85710 009 2

PiXZ Books
Halsgrove House, Ryelands Industrial Estate,
Bagley Road, Wellington, Somerset TA21 9PZ
Tel: 01823 653777
Fax: 01823 216796
email: sales@halsgrove.com

An imprint of Halstar Ltd, part of the Halsgrove group of companies
Information on all Halsgrove titles is available at: www.halsgrove.com

Printed and bound in China by Toppan Leefung Printing Ltd

Contents

How to use this book

The Area

The Northumbrian coastline, from the mouth of the Tyne to Berwick upon Tweed, has its share of craggy cliffs and long, sandy beaches. Yet once one moves beyond the Tyneside conurbation in the south, it has the feel of a neglected beauty. It has to compete with the Lake District to the west, while it is bypassed by those speeding north into Scotland.

Nevertheless, it caters for the connoisseur, and its stunning set pieces have not gone unnoticed by film makers.

Underlying the whole are the sandstone and limestone rocks that date back to the Carboniferous period, more than 300 million years ago. It was then that the coal deposits were laid down, which were mined to fuel the Industrial Revolution that became synonymous with the north-east of England.

Much of the scenery of the Northumbrian coast derives from this industrial legacy, as everywhere can be seen the quarries from which the coal and limestone were harvested. In most places, these have been reclaimed by Nature, and are now thriving wildlife reserves.

Toward the end of the Carboniferous, around 295 million years ago, volcanic magma forced its way through the sedimentary layers to create the dolerite of the Great Whin Sill, which lies exposed at intervals along the coast. The most prominent of these outcrops provided defendable heights during the Celtic and Saxon eras, when early Christianity struggled to survive against frequent Viking raids. As the Middle Ages progressed, these heights were appropriated as plinths for the great Norman castles from which conflict with Scotland was maintained.

Even into the modern era, relics of conflict dot the coast, in the many concrete pillboxes, anti-tank blocks and gun emplacements built to defend the country from possible invasion during the 1940s.

Now, however, Northumberland is peaceful, and its coastline is a long stretch of quiet retreat.

The Routes

The walks, varying in length from 2 to 5 miles, together cover the full spectrum of what the coast has to offer. They can each be enjoyed during half-a-day, or combined with a few hours on a beach, and in most cases could be conveniently shortened without loss of essential character.

As most of the walks follow level footpaths, with few, and only short uphill sections, the differences in difficulty are due to their lengths. They take circular routes and are all suitable for families, though small children will need to be carried in a backpack.

The starts of most walks can be reached by public transport. The Druridge Bay walks can be joined at points other than the described starts, if public transport be used. The two most northerly walks are more problematic. That on Lindisfarne is dependent upon tides, while the Cocklawburn walk is not accessible by public transport.

Starting points are given as Ordnance Survey grid references, and routes follow public rights-of-way. Directions specify compass points as follows: N (north), NNE (north-north-east), NE (northeast), ENE (east-north-east), E (east), ESE (east-southeast), SE (southeast), SSE (south-southeast), S (south), SSW (south-southwest), SW (southwest), WSW (west-southwest), W (west), WNW (west-northwest), NW (northwest) and NNW (north-northwest).

While the terrain is generally easy, remember that footpaths can become slippery when wet, cliff edges unstable and coastal weather fickle and often blustery. Wear appropriate footwear and carry windproof/waterproof clothing.

The Maps

The routes are easy to follow and you are unlikely to get lost. The route maps, however, should be seen as only rough guides. A more detailed map may be needed to locate the start of each walk. The north-east coast is covered by three Ordnance Survey maps in the Landranger series: 88 (Newcastle upon Tyne), 81 (Alnwick and Morpeth) and 75 (Berwick upon Tweed).

Key to Symbols Used

Level of difficulty:

Easy 🐚

Fair 🐚 🐚

More challenging 🐚 🐚 🐚

Map symbols:

🚗 Park & start

Tarred Road

- - - - Footpath

■ Building / Town

+ Church

🪣 Pub

▲ Landmark

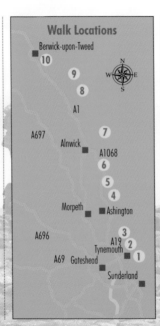

Walk Locations

Berwick-upon-Tweed
10
9
8
A1
A697
7
Alnwick
A1068
6
5
4
Morpeth ■ Ashington
A696
3
A19
2
Tynemouth
A69 Gateshead 1
Sunderland

1 North Shields and Tynemouth

A 3-mile walk along the final reaches of the River Tyne and the rocky headlands to the north.

Sharpness Point

Black Middens

Fish Quay

Strictly speaking, Tynemouth and North Shields no longer belong to Northumberland. Since 1974, they have been part of the Metropolitain Borough of North Tyneside, within the county of Tyne and Wear. However, they lie inside the historic boundary of Northumberland, and in a geographical sense, the River Tyne constitutes the logical southern limit of the county. The walk is essentially urban in character, but, in addition to much significant history, encompasses some impressive cliff and beach scenery as well as wonderful panoramic views of the river that became synonymous with the Industrial Revolution.

Level: 🐾 🐾
Length: 3 miles
Terrain: Roadside pavements and a concrete riverside promenade.
Park & Start: Tynemouth Metro Station.
Start Ref: NZ 366693
Public transport: Excellent Metro and bus services from Newcastle.
Websites: http://www.northtyneside. gov.uk
www.northtyneside.gov.uk

Buoy at start of promenade

① On exiting from Tynemouth Station, turn right (S) and follow the road, which curves round for 200 metres to a junction with Tynemouth Road. Turn right (SW) and follow this, passing the Master Mariners Home after 400 metres. Continue past the boundary sign for North Shields, and go downhill for 200 metres. Cross the road and go left (S) under the railway bridge onto Tanners Bank.

Mouth of the River Tyne

② At the bottom of the bank, swing right (SSW) onto Union Road. On the left side of this is the wall of the Fish Market, while on the right, the road is lined with restaurants and cafes, specialising in fish. At the end of Union Road is the open quayside, from which you can look across a small harbour called The Gut, toward the famous North Shields Fish Quay.

③ Retrace your steps along Union Road and turn right (E) onto Clifford Street and go along that, past the site of Clifford Fort. At the end of the street, go left (N) and past more fish merchants' premises, then turn right to reach the river beside a large red buoy.

The four cannons that adorn the base of the Collingwood Monument come from the Admiral's ship, the Royal Sovereign, on which he fought at Trafalgar.

Collingwood Monument

Cullercoats Long Sands

North Shields
Fish Quay

The comedian, Stan Laurel lived for a time in North Shields, before he moved on to Hollywood and fame. His sojourn is commemorated by a statue in Dockwray Square.

4 Move onto the promenade alongside the Low Lights car park, and follow this for 1000 metres,

Clifford's Fort was built in 1662 as a defence against the Dutch. It also saw use during the Napoleonic Wars.

as it curves gently from north to east. If the tide is out, the rocky shores of the Tyne will be uncovered, including the notorious Black Middens, which have been responsible for the demise of many fine ships. The rocks will be populated by large flocks of sea birds, mainly gulls, but with a scattering of cormorants.

5 Where the promenade swings to the left, take the surfaced footpath uphill for 200 metres to reach the Collingwood Monument. This commemorates Newcastle-born Admiral Lord Collingwood, who in 1805, led the British fleet into battle at Trafalgar.

6 Return downhill to the promenade and follow it for a further 50 metres to its end. Go uphill

North Shields grew up in the 12th century as a fishing village serving the Priory at Tynemouth Castle. The name 'Shields' comes from the shielings, or huts in which the fisher folk lived.

to the car park and stunning views, of the Tyne to the south-west, and Tynemouth Castle to the north, across the small bay of Prior's Haven, now home to the Tynemouth Sailing Club. The full lengths are also visible of the 800-metre North Pier and 1300-metre South Pier, which together shelter the final outflow of the river into the North Sea.

Master Mariners House

Tynemouth Castle was founded as a Benedictine monastery in 1090 AD. Later fortified, it continuously guarded the mouth of the Tyne against invasion, until as recently as 1960.

Promenade and Black Middens rocks

7 Follow the road from the car park (NNW) around the west of the bay, then carry on uphill for 200 metres, past the castle and the Gibraltar Rock Hotel, and follow the road around the rim of King Edward's Bay, which is almost enclosed by tall cliffs. On windy days, the waves are amplified by being funnelled into the bay, making this a popular venue for surfers.

8 Continue around the next rocky headland for 300 metres to the southern tip of Long Sands Beach, which runs for a kilometre as far as the former fishing village of Cullercoats. Beneath you is the now-abandoned open-air swimming pool.

9 The road now curves round to the west, and in a further 200 metres comes to a roundabout. Cross the road and turn left (S) onto Percy Park Road, which leads, in 500 metres, to the western end of Tynemouth's main street, opposite the former church, which is now a shopping centre, known as The Land of Green Ginger.

10 Continue south past this, and after 100 metres, turn right (W) to return to the Metro station.

2 **Whitley Bay**

A pleasant 3.5-mile walk along the sea front of a faded, yet still attractive seaside resort.

Though much smaller, Whitley Bay once rivalled Blackpool as a holiday destination for people from northern England and southern Scotland. The Spanish City was built in 1910 as a permanent fairground, and throughout the 20th century, it thrived. But from the 1980s, like most other resorts, it began a slow decline. Now, all that remains are the Dome and a small row of amusement arcades, cafés and chip shops on the adjacent Marine Avenue. However, regeneration is under way, and the sea front is once again an attractive venue for a walk or a day at the beach.

St Mary's Island, when accessible, is a rock-pool wonderland. Its lighthouse,

Level: ♥ ♥
Length: 3.5 miles
Terrain: Roadside pavements, concrete promenade and sandy beach. Uneven rocks if St Mary's Island is explored.
Park & start: Sea front car park on The Links, Whitley Bay.
Start ref.: NZ 351729
Public transport: Excellent Metro and bus services from Newcastle.
Websites: http://www.whitleybayonline.com
www.whitleybayonline.com
http://www.friendsofstmarysisland.co.uk
www.friendsofstmarysisland.co.uk

now a tourist attraction, and well worth a visit, began operating in 1898, replacing a much older one that stood at Tynemouth Priory.

13

1 Turn right out of the car park, go over the pedestrian crossing to the pavement that runs along Whitley Bay Links. Follow the road for 200 metres, past the site of Spanish City, marked by its white Dome. Continue past the flower park and down onto the beach.

2 Turn left (N) past the Boardwalk Bistro, and after 50 metres, go up the steps onto the North Promenade. You could continue along the beach if you so prefer, and join the promenade farther on, up one

The Dome of the Spanish City became a Grade II listed building in 1986, because of its early use of reinforced concrete.

Rendezvous café

of the several sets of steps leading at intervals from the beach.

3 After 400 metres, you will pass a skateboard and BMX park that was opened in 2008. 200 metres beyond this is a now-disused fountain, erected in 1937 to celebrate the Coronation of King George VI and Queen Elizabeth. A further 100 metres brings you to the Rendezvous Café, which continues to serve ice creams

The Spanish City is mentioned in the 1980 song, 'Tunnel of Love', by Mark Knopfler and Dire Straits. It also appears briefly in the 1976 film, 'The Likely Lads'.

and light refreshments while clinging doggedly to the faded charm of the Whitley Bay of the 1950s.

4 Another 200 metres takes you past a small dene, to the end of the promenade. Continue along the beach, or ascend to a footpath that runs along the edge of the mud cliff, past the deeper ravine of Brierdene. The next promenade, accessed by a set of steps, is reached after 800 metres.

5 Follow this round to the car park at Curry's Point, from which a short descent leads to the causeway to St Mary's Island.

6 If the tide is out, cross the causeway, past numerous rock pools that are home to whelks, periwinkles, sea anemones and hermit

Anchor, St Mary's Island

St Mary's Island from causeway

Dome, Spanish City

crabs, to the island. The Visitor Centre is open most of the time, and for a small fee, you can ascend the 137 steps, (the last 20 of which are of ladder steepness), to the top of the lighthouse, to enjoy a superb view of the coastline, from Tynemouth in the south to Blyth in the north.

St Mary's Island was used in 1995 as the location for the ITV programme, 'Five go to Demon's Rock', based on an Enid Blyton story.

Optic, St Mary's Island lighthouse

(7) Having enjoyed a leisurely hour-or-more on the island, return over the causeway. Take the higher road from Curry's Point, which curves to a second car park at 300 metres. Behind this is a wall containing openings that permit views across

17

Flower garden near sea front opposite Dome

St Mary's Wetland, where there are likely to be a variety of water birds. 200 metres farther, you will join the main road from Whitley Bay to Seaton Sluice.

8 Turn left (S) onto the pavement and follow it for a mile (1600 metres), past the golf course, Brierdene, two smaller denes and the Rendezvous Café, back to the start.

The original optic of St Mary's Island lighthouse weighed 7 tonnes and was one of the biggest of its time. It is now in a museum in Penzance. The present assembly weighs 2.5 tonnes and was installed in 1988 to coincide with the lighthouse's 90th birthday.

Promenade and St Mary's Island

3 **Seaton Sluice**

A highly-varied 2-mile walk that encompasses cliff scenery, industrial history and a nature reserve.

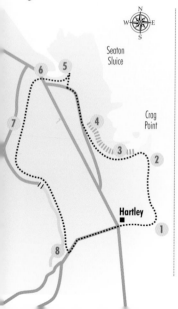

Level:

Length: 2 miles.

Terrain: Grassy footpaths and roadside pavements.

Park & start: Car park behind Delaval Arms Hotel, at roundabout on A193 at southern end of Seaton Sluice.

Start ref.: NZ 344758

Public transport: Excellent bus service from Newcastle.

Websites: http://www.seaton-sluice.co.uk
www.seaton-sluice.co.uk

The residential nature of the housing between Old Hartley and Seaton Sluice hides a history of mining and other less well-known industries that is far from obvious. The visitor driving along the main road from Whitley Bay to Blyth would also be unaware of the proximity of a quite dramatic, though short section of Northumbrian coast. The promontory of Crag Point is composed of steep, even overhanging sandstone faces topped by crumbly shale. At low tide, the boulder-strewn base of the crag can be negotiated, making the faces accessible to rock climbers, who sometimes come here to practise.

Holywell Dene

19

1 From the car park behind the Delaval Arms, follow the footpath leading from the north-east corner, that runs adjacent to a caravan park. At a fork in the track, take the right footpath, which runs along the edge of the cliffs. Take care, as the cliff top can be unstable in places.

Seaton Sluice's industrial history, reaches back to the thirteenth century, and includes salt production, coal export and glass manufacture.

Beneath the cliffs are extensive horizontal beds of sandstone, which are exposed at low tide. Birds that you might see here include oystercatchers, cormorants, gulls, lapwings and occasionally curlews.

2 Continue for 200 metres to Crag Point, the top of which is marked by a wooden post carrying a lifebelt. With care, it is possible to descend to the flat top of the cliff, which gives some impressive views of the nearby coastline. Past Crag Point, the main footpath is resumed.

The hills that surround the harbour are composed largely of sand, chalk and flint, carried as ballast by ships on their journey from London, prior to their collection of a cargo of coal.

Seaton Sluice Harbour

Crag Point and Old Hartley

(4) Turn right (N) onto the pavement. The beach below, part sandy, part rocky, is dominated by a huge boulder, known as Charlie's Rock. Its companion was blown up some years ago when it became dangerously unstable.

(5) Continue for 500 metres to the harbour at Seaton Sluice. The original entrance lies to the north, but a second one, The Cut, was dug through solid sandstone to the east, in 1761. The Cut is 270 metres long, 9 metres wide and around 5 metres deep. The small footbridge occupies the place of the original swing bridge, which was rotated to allow the passage of taller-masted ships. Continue (W) for 200 metres along

(3) Where this broadens into a concrete roadway, take a grassy footpath to the right, which follows a fence along the rim of the, now lower, cliffs to join the road at a wooden seat.

At the peak of glass-making at Seaton Sluice, the bottle works employed 63 workers and manufactured 145,000 dozen bottles in a year.

The Cut, Seaton Sluice

The mouth of Seaton Burn was always a natural harbour, but suffered from silting. A new harbour was commissioned by Lord Delaval in 1660, and thirty years later, the sluice gates, from which the village derives its name, were added to aid in the removal of silt.

the edge of the harbour, past The Octagon, the eighteenth century Harbour Masters' office, where excise duties were levied, and the adjacent Waterford Arms, to the main road.

6   Cross the road and follow the track down to the right of St Paul's church, into Holywell Dene. This is the site of the Old Harbour, and is still home to many small boats. The Dene has been a Local Nature Reserve since 2003, and comprises salt marsh, woodland and wetland habitats. More than fifty bird species are regularly recorded here.

Charlie's Rock

7 Continue (S) along the footpath following the eastern edge of the Dene, through hawthorn, blackthorn and sycamore, which opens onto a small car park on the edge of Old Hartley. This consists largely of private housing today, but stands on the site of a former mining village. In 1862, miners from here and New Hartley, two miles to the north-west lost their lives in one of the worst disasters in British mining history.

The Hartley Pit disaster of 1862, caused by blockage of the entrance shaft, led to the deaths of 204 men and boys, through suffocation. It resulted in legislation making it compulsory for all mines to have two separate shafts.

Cliffs at Crag Point

Rocky beach south of Crag Point

Seaton Sluice Harbour

8 Turn left (ENE) onto the pavement and go gently uphill, past the remains of a railway bridge, to the roundabout. Cross the road to the Delaval Arms Hotel and continue past this to the car park at the top of the cliffs.

4 Druridge Bay (South)

A 5-mile exploration of important wetland bird sanctuaries followed by a return along arguably the finest of Northumberland's beaches.

The coastline of Northumberland is characterised more by shallow-curved bays than by jagged indentations. The longest, and perhaps finest of these bays, Druridge, runs for six miles from Cresswell in the south to Low Hauxley in the north. The full stretch of the bay comprises a succession of sand dunes, behind which are a series of important wetland nature reserves, created from former opencast coal mines that ran along the coast. Though popular, Druridge is long enough, and sufficiently far from centres of population never to become crowded.

Level: 🐾 🐾
Length: 5 miles
Terrain: Rough-surfaced track and grassy footpaths.
Park & start: Southern end of Druridge Links, just where minor road from Cresswell to Widdrington takes a sharp left (W) turn. One can shorten the walk by parking farther north on the Links.
Start ref.: NZ 277960
Public transport: The Arriva bus No. 518 from Morpeth to Alnwick stops at Widdrington. A footpath leads east for 1200 metres to Low Chibburn.
Websites: http://www.visitnorthumberland.com
www.visitnorthumberland.com

Greylag geese, northern lake, East Chevington nature reserve

Low Chibburn ruin

 1 Walk north along the Druridge Links road. The shrubbery to your left hides the Druridge Pools Nature Reserve.

2 After 400 metres, a detour (W), marked by a signpost pointing to Chibburn Ruin and Widdrington Village leads through shrubs and along a wooden board-walk between high banks. Seasonal pools that line the sides of the path provide a refuge for frogs and great crested newts.

3 A small hide to the left over-looks shallow pools, while a second, more substantial one to the right opens a view across the largest of the pools, an important site for both resident and migrant birds. Otters can also be seen here. Continue beyond the hides for 200 metres to a stile.

4 Cross the stile and follow the right hand fence along the

Druridge Pools occupy the site of Radar North opencast mine, which operated from 1957 to 1973. The East Chevington mine was worked between 1983 and 1994.

side of the field. Continue to follow the right-of-way over a series of stiles and a farm road until you come to the ruins of Low Chibburn, that date back to the 14th century.

Druridge Pool nature reserve

Druridge Bay

5 After exploring the ruins, return to the last stile, cross this and turn left (N) onto the farm road that leads, after 200 metres, to a cross-roads at the corner of a wood. Turn right (ENE) and follow the road for 750 metres to a junction with the footpath behind the dunes.

A mile from the southern end of Druridge Bay is the site of the former Ellington Colliery, which closed in 2005. It was the last deep coal mine in the north-east of England and the last in the UK to extract coal from beneath the sea.

6 Turn left (N) and follow this between the dunes and rough pastureland. Along the roadsides are wild flowers. Some are coastal specialties, others have taken advantage of the poor soils of the open cast workings to establish themselves in place of less resilient species.

7 You will come to a footpath leading to the left. Follow this to the edge of a narrow wood, then turn right, and right again, to reach a large pond, surrounded by tall reeds, which hide it completely from the main pathway. This is the beginning of the East Chevington Nature Reserve. One of the Northumberland Wildlife Trust's most recent, it was acquired in 2003, following reclamation of the former opencast site

8 The footpath runs back along the southern shore of the pond to re-join the main track just before it crosses a narrow bridge. Go over the bridge and continue for about half-a-mile to the northern lake of East Chevington.

Low Chibburn was founded in 1313 by the Knights Hospitallers, who gave refuge to pilgrims on their way to Lindisfarne. The buildings were burned by a small, opportunist French force in 1691.

9 The first hide gives a view over the full length of the lake, one of Northumberland's most important bird-watching sites. The second hide, situated half-way along the eastern shore, looks out across a small archipelago, and will bring you much closer to the birds, which include greylag and pink-footed geese, ducks, waders, and in winter, migrants from the Arctic.

10 Go back to the main footpath and return to the bridge at the southern end of the first East Chevington lake and cross it to the southern side of the waterway. The sound of breakers will remind you of the proximity of the sea shore, just over the dunes.

11 Cross the dunes and stroll at leisure along one of the finest beaches in the north of England. There are several passages through the dunes. Choose any convenient one for your return to your transport.

Birds, northern lake, East Chevington nature reserve

5 Druridge Bay North and Country Park

A 2.75-mile family walk that includes the Druridge Bay Country Park.

Like the other pools of similar open-cast origin, Ladyburn Lake provides a home for bird life, but its main purpose is as a centre for leisure activities. Sailing is permitted on the lake. There is a network of walking trails and cycle tracks punctuated by picnic areas. Near the Visitor Centre is a children's play area, while the centre itself houses an impressive display illustrating the geology, wildlife and history of Druridge Bay. The Visitor Centre is open at weekends throughout the year, on Bank Holidays and daily during local school holidays.

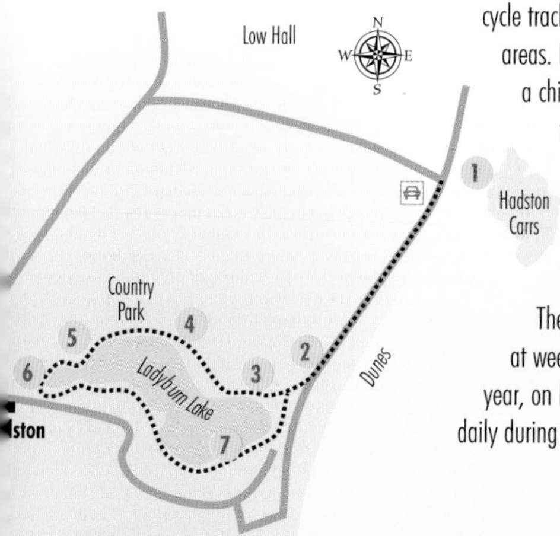

Level: 🖤
Length: 2.75 miles
Terrain: Tarred road, rough-surfaced track and grassy footpath.
Park & start: Hadston Scaurs car park, at eastern end of minor road that runs east from A1068, 1.75 miles south of Amble.
Start ref.: NU 279009
Public transport: The Arriva Morpeth – Alnwick bus No. 518 stops at Hadston, 10 minutes' walk from the Country Park.
Websites: http://www.northumber lanlife.org/druridgebaycountrypark
www.northumberlandlife.org/druridge baycountrypark

Map labels: Low Hall, Hadston Carrs, Country Park, Ladyburn Lake, Dunes, ston, 1, 2, 3, 4, 5, 6, 7

1 Follow the road south, past fields on the right and World War II concrete structures amid the dunes on the left. Along the dunes are dense thickets of gorse, willow and hawthorn.

2 After 800 metres, you come to the corner of a wood, made up of sycamore, blackthorn, ash and conifers. 200 metres farther, a footpath enters the wood. Follow this as it snakes through the trees for another

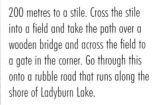

During World War II, Druridge Bay was used for target practice by the Royal Air Force. The concrete structures were built as shelters for the observers.

200 metres to a stile. Cross the stile into a field and take the path over a wooden bridge and across the field to a gate in the corner. Go through this onto a rubble road that runs along the shore of Ladyburn Lake.

3 Turn right (W) and continue for 50 metres to a bridge, which carries you for a similar distance over a weir. 10 metres beyond the bridge, the track forks. Take the right fork, which leads into Coldrife

Runners competing in triathlon, Druridge Bay Country Park

Ford and stepping stones

Stone Age middens, dating back 8500 years have been found among the dunes of the northern end of Druridge Bay. Bronze Age burial sites, from 3500 years ago have been found in the same area.

Wood. The path curves through the wood for 250 metres and ends at right angles to the shore, where it joins with the left fork.

4 Turn right (W), through the gate, and follow the path, which now runs along the shore, past

more patches of woodland and through a succession of gates to the western end of the lake.

5 A ford, lined with a row of stepping stones, separates the main lake from a smaller one to the west. A small nature sanctuary runs along the northern shore of this smaller pond. Go through the gate into the sanctuary and continue to the end, where you turn left (S) over a Chinese bridge.

During the 1980s, Druridge Bay was proposed as the site for a nuclear power station. A vigorous campaign was mounted against this, and the proposal was abandoned in 1989.

Stile leading to lake

Ladyburn Lake

6 Go up a short slope and swing left to join a track that leads up from the ford and stepping stones. Continue eastwards, past a swan-sculpture seat, to the next gate, then take a narrower footpath that runs along the southern shore, past a sailing ramp, and leads eventually to the Visitor Centre.

The Druridge Bay Country Park and Ladyburn Lake occupy the site of the former Coldrife open cast colliery, which operated from 1966 to 1971.

Boats on lake

7 Return to the lakeshore and continue along it to join the lakeside rubble track. On joining it, turn right, then immediately left onto a cycle track. This leads through the wood and back onto the beach road, which is followed north for 1000 metres back to the starting point.

Cyclists competing in triathlon, Druridge Bay Country Park

Chinese bridge

6 Warkworth

A varied 3-mile walk that takes in coastal sand dunes, a golf course, a riverside and a castle-dominated village.

Human occupation at Warkworth dates from Neolithic times, as demonstrated by cup-and-ring carvings

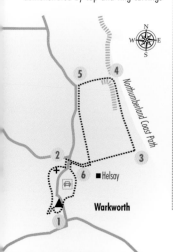

Warkworth

■ Helsay

Northumberland Coast Path

on crags above the riverbank. From the 8th century AD, it was the site of an Anglo-Saxon religious community. The castle was built in the loop of the river in the 12th century, when Henry II granted the region to Roger fitzEustace, and later extended. In the 14th century, it was acquired by the Percy family, who dominated Northumbrian history for the next 500 years. The castle played its part in the Anglo-Scottish wars, the Wars of the Roses and the political intrigues of that turbulent period. The lion emblem of the Percys can be seen on the north wall of the castle, overlooking the town.

Level: 🥾 🥾
Length: 3 miles.
Terrain: Rough-surfaced track and sandy footpath.
Park & start: English Heritage car park at entrance to Warkworth Castle.
Start ref.: NU 246057
Public transport: Buses from Morpeth and Alnwick.
Websites: http://www.english-heritage.org.uk
www.english-heritage.org.uk

Warkworth from the castle

(1) From the western end of the car park, descend a set of steps, and follow the footpath north along the side of the castle to a sign pointing to Warkworth Hermitage. Turn sharp left and descend to the riverside. Turn back right (N) and follow the river to the northern reach of the loop, and St Lawrence's church.

In the market place of Warkworth, in 1701, The Old Pretender, James Stuart, the son of the deposed James II, was proclaimed James III of England (and VIII of Scotland).

World War II concrete blocks on beach

Half-a-mile upstream of the castle is The Hermitage, an ornately-carved chapel and inner chamber cut, in 1400 AD, cave-like, out of the rock of the riverbank.

2 Continue to the Old Bridge, and cross this to the northern bank. Cross over the main road and follow the minor road (ENE) that leads uphill toward the golf club and beach. The pavement gives way to a broad grass verge, which is followed for 400 metres to the Coquet Leisure Park. Take the public bridleway toward the coast path. This runs downhill, past the golf course to the sand dunes.

River Coquet and Warkworth Castle

3 On reaching the dunes, turn left (N) onto a narrow footpath, signposted toward Alnmouth. This runs for a kilometre between the golf course and the dunes, then winds between hills and through thickets of blackthorn, bramble and roses to converge onto the beach at the mouth of a dene. Farther along the beach are a series of concrete blocks, relics of World War II coastal defences.

The Old Bridge, constructed in the 14th century, was in continual use carrying traffic until 1965, when it was replaced by the modern road bridge.

4 Turn left (W) and follow the path through the dene and under the bridge. 100 metres beyond the bridge, walk across another section of golf course, go through a gate and onto a rubble track. Follow this for 250 metres until you reach a cycle track that runs adjacent and parallel to the main road.

St Lawrence's Church

Sundial, St Lawrence's Church

5 Turn left (S) onto the cycle track. After 200 metres, it diverges from the main road and continues for 700 metres to join the beach road you followed earlier. Turn right (WSW) and go down the hill for 200 metres to the road bridge over the river. Turn left and cross the bridge, then turn left again onto The Butts.

The Old Bridge is one of the few remaining fortified bridges in England. Its gatehouse was once used as a prison.

Bridge over the dene

New Bridge over Coquet · Old Bridge

6 Follow the road and river round to the south. At the end of the road, go right and up the steps past the Sun Inn. Cross the road and go left to the Castle car park.

The 12th century St Lawrence's Church retains its original Norman pillars, windows and oak beams. A church has stood on the same site since 737 AD.

Old Bridge

7 Craster and Dunstanburgh Castle

A 4.5-mile walk past one of Northumberland's most wildly-situated ruins, and its quieter rural hinterland.

Level: 🖤
Length: 4.5 miles.
Terrain: Grassy and sandy footpaths, tarred road.
Park & start: Car park at entrance to Craster village.
Start ref.: NU 256197
Public transport: 501 bus service from Alnwick.
Websites: http://www.english-heritage.org.uk
www.english-heritage.org.uk

Dunstanburgh Castle stands on a windswept promontory of the Great Whin Sill. Though ruined, its walls encompass the largest area of any castle in Northumberland. Its situation is so wildly impressive that Turner was inspired to paint it several times. Construction of the castle was begun in 1313, by Thomas Plantagenet, a cousin of King Edward II. He later rebelled against the king, and was executed in 1322. During the 1380s, it was acquired by John of Gaunt, and supported the Lancastrian cause during the Wars of the Roses, though it twice succumbed to siege by the Yorkists.

Dunstanburgh Castle on a windy day

41

Greymare Rock

1 Turn right (E) out of the car park and follow the road into Craster village. On reaching the harbour, turn left (N) along Dunstanburgh Road and go through the gate toward the castle.

Craster village takes its name from William de Crauceter, whose family held the estate from the 13th century.

2 The grassy footpath runs for 2 kilometres, through large clumps of gorse and a series of gates. In contrast to the many sandy beaches in Northumberland, this one is rocky, its shore composed of hard, black dolerite. On the final stretch the path swings to the right and up a short hill before rising gently to the castle gate.

Lobster pots, Craster Harbour

3 Follow the track to the left (W) of the castle. Below is a reed-fringed pond, known as The Mere. The path descends to the north of the castle and leads through a gate into the golf course. On the right is a wonderfully contorted piece of

The tiny fishing village of Craster is famous for its kippers, which are still smoked over oak shavings in traditional smoke houses in the village.

Limekiln

Dedication plaque, Craster Harbour

stratified carboniferous limestone, known as the Greymare Rock.

4 Continue along the edge of the golf course, past a concrete World War II pill box. The beach beyond here changes to the more usual sandy shore, fringed by dunes. Carry on through the dunes, cross a small wooden bridge over a dene, and go up a set of steps to a second pill box. 50 metres beyond this, take the path that leads away from the beach to a small car park.

Dunstanburgh Castle is said to be haunted by a 16th century knight, Sir Guy the Seeker, who searches the grounds for a hidden room in which lies a sleeping beauty.

5 Take the road that runs south-west toward Dunstan Steads farm. After 100 metres, there is a footpath leading left (SE) to the castle, which provides an option if you wish to shorten the walk. Alternatively, carry on for a further 100 metres to the farm, then turn left (S) onto the bridleway and cycle track through the farm.

Dunstanburgh Castle

6 Follow the surfaced road for a little over a mile (1700 metres) past a barn and a small wood, at the side of which stand a lime kiln and two pill boxes.

Craster – village and harbour

The Mere was formed by flooding of the fields below the castle in the 16th century. It often becomes flooded again during periods of heavy rainfall.

Turrets, Dunstanburgh Castle

7 On reaching Dunstan Square farm, turn left (ENE) through a gate and cross the side of a field for 300 metres to a gate. Go through this and up a hill between gorse forests. Descend to a stile, cross this and take a diagonal track downhill to the right to the next gate. Go through this and continue south for 1 kilometre back into Craster.

8 Bamburgh

A 4-mile beach walk overlooked by one of Britain's most impressive, and impressively-situated castles.

Bamburgh Castle, standing on its 60-metre-high plinth of Whin Sill dolerite, is so huge that it can be seen from several miles away in almost any direction. The early Saxon wooden fort was replaced by the Normans in the 12th century. It suffered much destruc-tion during the Wars of the Roses and fell into neglect. In the 1750s, it was partly restored by Lord Crewe. In the 19th century, it was acquired by the Victorian industrialist, Lord Armstrong, who built it up to its present magnificence, which is enjoyed by his descendents, who continue to reside in the castle.

Level: 🥾 🥾
Length: 4 miles.
Terrain: Sandy and rocky stretches of beach, grassy footpath, surfaced road.
Park & start: Car park to south of Bamburgh Castle.
Start ref.: NU 183349
Public transport: Good bus service from Newcastle, Morpeth and Alnwick.
Websites: http://www.visitnorthumber land.com
www.visitnorthumberland.com

Grace Darling's tomb, Bamburgh

1 From the car park, cross the road and go up the rough track opposite, to the Castle car park. Follow any one of the variety of paths through the dunes and onto the beach. Turn left (NW) and walk along the beach beneath the castle.

Bamburgh Castle from dunes

The 7th or 8th century Bamburgh sword, discovered in 1960 by archaeologists in the castle, is of such unusual construction, comprising six strands of bonded iron, that it is thought to be unique in the world.

2 After 800 metres, the sand gives way to rocks, composed of Whin Sill dolerite. Continue over the rocks, past a series of World War II concrete defensive blocks, two of which have been painted to resemble dice. Near the lighthouse, a stratum of carboniferous limestone can be seen beneath the dolerite.

Bamburgh beach

Bamburgh Castle has provided the backdrop to scenes in several films, including 'Becket', 'Macbeth', 'El Cid', 'Mary Queen of Scots' and 'King Arthur.'

World War II concrete blocks

Bamburgh Castle from beach

(3) A grassy track leads round to the west of the lighthouse, Alternatively, you could scramble over the rocks above the tide. Beyond the lighthouse, either continue along the beach, or if the tide precludes that, follow the grassy footpath along the foot of the dunes, in a generally WNW direction, for 1400 metres to Budle Point.

(4) Swing left (SW) around the Point and follow the southern edge of the broad expanse of Budle Bay. The dunes along this stretch are more sandy than previously, and reach farther from the beach.

Inner Farne Island from beach

5 After 600 metres, you will come to the remains of a concrete jetty. Turn left (S) at this and go through the dunes, where you will meet a track that leads past the eastern fence of a caravan park, and up to a World War II gun emplacement. Turn sharp right at this and go uphill to reach a golf course. Turn left (NE) and follow the bridleway that runs between the golf course and the top of the sand dunes. The route is marked by a series of blue poles.

In 1838, the 22-year-old Grace Darling, from Bamburgh, braved a storm in a rowing boat to rescue survivors of the SS Forfarshire, wrecked on one of the Farne Islands.

Budle Bay from WW II gun emplacement

The church is the Grace Darling Museum, which is also worth a visit.

8 Return to the town and continue back to the car park beneath the Castle.

The walled garden in Bamburgh, was built in 1693, using bricks brought to Budle Bay as ballast in ships.

6 The track meanders from a north-easterly to an easterly direction for 1200 metres, becoming more well-defined past Budle Point, until it comes to the Golf Club House.

7 From here, a surfaced road leads SE back into Bamburgh. On reaching the first houses, continue along The Wynding and into the town. It is worth turning right here to visit St Aidan's Church, in the grounds of which is the tomb of local heroine, Grace Darling. Opposite

Kite surfing, Budle Bay

9 Lindisfarne

A 4-mile walk around Holy Island, that captures the scenery, wildlife and history of the Northumbrian coast in a nutshell.

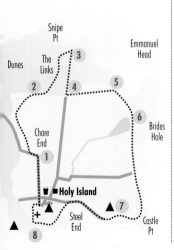

In 635 AD, King Oswald of Northumbria invited St Aidan, from the monastic settlement on Iona, to found a monastery on Lindisfarne. Aidan's death, in 651, coincided with the vocation of shepherd boy, Cuthbert, who became Bishop of Lindisfarne. On his death in 687, Cuthbert was buried on the island, but 200 years later, following Viking raids, monks carried his body throughout northern England and southern Scotland for seven years before reburial in Chester-le-Street. In 995, he was finally reburied in Durham Cathedral. The present Priory was built during the 12th century.

Level: 🥾 🥾
Length: 4 miles
Terrain: Tarred road, rough-surfaced track and grassy and sandy footpaths.
Park & start: Large Pay-and-display car park to the north of Lindisfarne village.
Start ref.: NU 125425
Public transport: The daily Newcastle-Berwick coach service passes through Beal. Transport from there to the island is dependent upon the tides.
Websites: http://www.lindisfarne.org.uk www.lindisfarne.org.uk A study of the tide tables is crucial. Every few weeks, drivers become stranded by incoming tides on the causeway that links the island to the mainland.

Lindisfarne Castle

Lindisfarne is an important National Nature Reserve and wintering site for migrating birds, including whooper swans and Brent geese from Svalbard. Plants include the rare black bog rush and Lindisfarne helleborine.

1 Take the northern exit from the car park and walk west along the roadside for 150 metres, to a gate and notice board. On the sands in front of you is the end of the line of wooden posts marking the Pilgrims' Way from the mainland. Turn right (N) through the gate and follow the foot-path for 500 metres to a small hill. Take the right fork that curves round the base of the hill.

Lindisfarne Priory and Castle

2 When the track forks again, follow the left fork, through sand hills. When the land opens out beyond the hills, take any one of the many criss-crossing tracks that lead, in another 400 metres, to the high dunes that overlook the beach of Coves Haven. If there are seals around Lindisfarne, it is here that you are likely to see them. Turn right (SE) and follow the path along the top of the dunes to the western end of the limestone cliffs.

The Lindisfarne Gospels, an illuminated Latin manuscript, was created around 715 AD on Lindisfarne. It is one of the finest examples of Celtic-Saxon art, and is now housed in the British Library.

Lindisfarne Castle was originally a Tudor fort, but was redesigned as a private house for Edward Hudson, in 1903, by Sir Edwin Lutyens. The walled garden was designed between 1906 and 1912 by Gertrude Jekyll.

The six limekilns are the largest and best preserved in Northumberland. They were built in the 1860s by a Dundee firm. At one time, five boats carried coal and lime between Lindisfarne and Dundee.

3 Turn right, (S) and follow the path across reclaimed land that was once occupied by limestone quarries. Lindisfarne Castle can be seen in the distance. After 500 metres, you will come to a gate.

4 Turn left (E) and follow the path alongside the fence. On reaching a wall, continue along this to a second gate, beside a notice board.

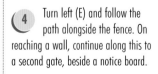

(5) Go through the gate onto a raised track, that was once a waggonway, carrying limestone from the quarries. This brings you, in 400 metres, to The Lough, which is over-looked by a bird-watching hide.

(6) Continue for another kilo-metre, as the track converges with the eastern shore of Lindisfarne. It then curves to the right (W), past limekilns and around the base of the dolerite crag on which stands the castle. 100 metres to the north of this is a small walled garden.

Lindisfarne Castle was used as the location for Roman Polanski's 1966 film, 'Cul-de-Sac'. It also appears in the 1983 television film, 'The Scarlet Pimpernel'.

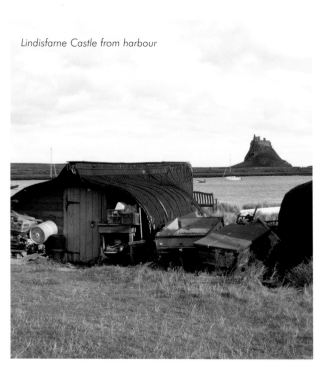

Lindisfarne Castle from harbour

Lindisfarne – harbour and castle

Lindisfarne Castle

7 100 metres beyond the castle, go through the gate and follow the road toward the village. On reaching a footpath, follow this south, past upturned boats, now employed as storage huts by fishermen. The footpath curves past more huts and ascends a hill, called The Heugh, that lies south of, and overlooks Lindisfarne Priory.

8 Continue along the path, which now descends over rocky ground to a beach, then curves back uphill, past the Church of St Mary the Virgin, and enters the village at The Priory. Turn left, (N) and zig-zag through the village to its northern end. 400 metres farther, you will return to the car park.

The Lough, bordered by reeds, reed mace and bogbean, was dug by the monks as a source of fresh water and fish.

10 **Cocklawburn Beach**

A 2-mile walk that includes a short stretch of the most northerly sandy beach in England.

This short, but geologically interesting walk begins at a fence that marks the boundary of the former

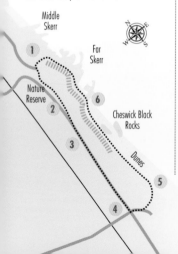

Cocklawburn Dunes nature reserve. Though it no longer exists as a discrete reserve, it remains a small part of the Berwickshire and North Northumberland Coast Special Area of Conservation, which stretches from the Scottish borders region, north of Berwick to Alnmouth in the south. The beach resembles some of the other Northumbrian beaches to the south, though it is far less well-known than they. Being close to the border, it is justly popular with visitors from Scotland.

Level:
Length: 2 miles
Terrain: Grassy footpath, surfaced road, sandy and rocky beach.
Park & start: At end of beach road that runs east from Scremerston, just off the A1 to the south of Berwick.
Start ref.: NU 032481
Public transport: None.
Websites: http://www.northumberland-cam.com/cheswick
www.northumberland-cam.com/cheswick

Dolerite rock on beach

Brachiopod Fossils

Eider ducks, the emblematic birds of Northumberland, were the beneficiaries of one of the first ever bird protection laws, instigated by St Cuthbert in 676 AD.

(1) Go through the gate in the fence and immediately, follow the footpath (S) to the top of the hill, which is occupied by a concrete World War II gun emplacement. The opening commands the coast as far as Lindisfarne, the castle of which can be seen on the southern skyline, along with Bamburgh Castle. Follow the raised trackway downhill through brambles and former limestone quarries.

(2) At the bottom of the hill, there are several tracks. Take the one which converges with the tarred cycle track adjacent to the fenced area, and climb over the stile in the corner, to join this. Follow the cycle track (SE) past a private fishing pond. Herons stalk the margins, while tufted ducks and little grebes fish the deeper stretches.

(3) Continue on the cycle track, through a gate, and in 500 metres, you will come to another gate at the end of a road leading from Cheswick village. In the western distance are the outlines of the Cheviot Hills.

Crinoid fossils are locally known as St Cuthbert's beads. When found on the beaches, during mediaeval times, they were often threaded together to form necklaces or rosaries.

4 Turn left (E) and follow the footpath for 150 metres through the sand dunes onto the beach. If the tide is out, you will see a small patch of dark-coloured rock in front of you. This is a tiny outlier, and probably the most northerly manifestation of the Great Whin Sill. It marks the start of a short, though geologically interesting stretch of what might otherwise be seen as just another sandy, dune-lined beach.

5 Turn left (N) and walk along the beach. The first substantial region of rocks are the Cheswick Black Rocks, comprising well defined layers of bedded sandstone. At the

Several gun emplacements were built along the Northumberland coast during WWII, as it was feared that this could be an area chosen for invasion by German troops.

tide's edge, you might see flocks of oystercatchers, ringed plovers, turnstones, sandpipers, redshanks and bar-tailed godwit. Floating on the swell there might also be eider ducks, while gannets could be dive-bombing shoals of fish.

6 The next large rocky section, known as Far Skerr, begins as sandstone, but changes, abruptly to an extensive, gently sloping limestone pavement. Here, and in the boulders that lie beneath the shale hills are

Berwick

numerous fossil crinoids, bivalves and brachiopods, which date back to the Carboniferous period of 299-350 million years ago, when this part of Britain was covered by a tropical sea.

If the tide is in, and the headland difficult to walk around, you can follow a footpath up the hill into the former nature reserve and back to the car park. Alternatively, go round the promontory, across the limestone beds and past the ruins of some limekilns. 150 metres to the north of the kilns, take a short track through the sand dunes, which brings you to the car park.

Eider ducks are sometimes known locally as 'Cuddy's ducks', Cuddy being a local diminutive of Cuthbert.

Ringed plovers